Setting Goals

Sandra Lee Smith

THE ROSEN PUBLISHING GROUP, INC.

NEW YORK

To my in-laws,
Ed and Flo Smith, Sr.,
who have been excellent role models
for success with goals.

Published in 1992 by The Rosen Publishing Group, Inc.
29 East 21st Street, New York, NY 10010

First Edition
Copyright 1992 by The Rosen Publishing Group, Inc.

Manufactured in the United States of America

Library of Congress Cataloging-in-Publication Data

Smith, Sandra Lee
    Setting goals / by Sandra Lee Smith
    (The Life skills library)
    Includes bibliographical references and index.
    Summary: Examines how people's values influence their goals and discusses how to set and achieve appropriate goals.
    ISBN 0-8239-1451-8
    1. Goals (Psychology)—Juvenile literature. 2. Values—Juvenile Literature.
[1. Conduct in life. 2. Goals (Psychology). 3. Values.] I. Title II. Series.
BF503.S55 1992
158'.1—dc20   92-15262
                                                                   CIP
                                                                    AC

CONTENTS

INTRODUCTION

One of the most impor-
tant life skills you can learn is that of setting goals.
Setting goals brings purpose to your life. Goals help
you fulfill your desires, maintain your values, manage your time, and succeed in your tasks and
projects. It is important to know where you are
headed. If you have no clear idea of your direction,
you can easily be led astray.

Think about the captain of a ship. Let's name him
Captain Jones and pretend he wants to sail to a
village on the coast of Alaska. To get there, he must
pass through a dangerous channel. There are many
large rocks in the channel. Some of the rocks are
below the surface of the water and hard to spot.

Captain Jones must be very careful as he navigates
his ship through the channel. Any wrong decision

—

It takes hard work and careful planning to become a winner.

or hasty move could end in disaster. He takes the risk, though, because he is carrying supplies to the village. An oil tanker had crashed on the rocks, and the oil spill had killed much of the sea life on which the people normally depended. Therefore they are suffering a severe shortage of food.

If Captain Jones does not make it, the villagers will starve. His goal is to sail to the village. He has a purpose in going there; the villagers need food.

Captain Brown and Captain Carson, on the other hand, do not have a goal or purpose for sailing to another village on the Alaskan coast. They just want to see what is there. They have heard that it is beautiful and the villagers are friendly. Perhaps they can make a trade agreement. Maybe they can bring tourists to the village.

All three ships set sail about the same time. Soon after they start, a storm hits. The wind tosses the ships about in the channel. All three captains are worried about the safety of their ships and crews. If the wind or waves toss them onto the rocks, they will be in the same mess that the oil tanker was in.

Because ships are very expensive, Captain Brown decides to cancel his trip. He really didn't have much reason to go. He only wanted to check out the village as a possible tourist site.

Captain Jones, however, has a very good reason to get to his village. The people need his cargo.

Captain Carson's motive is not that strong, but he enjoys a challenge and will risk the danger to see if he can make it through the storm to the village.

Captain Jones puts his full crew to work. He stays up all night to guide the ship. He puts in every bit of effort to bring his ship through the channel despite the weather.

Captain Jones makes it to the village. He set a goal and he fulfills it. In spite of the dangers, he goes onward. Why? Because it is important. He has a strong reason to go. People need him.

Captain Carson presses on also. He makes it through the storm, but he doesn't get to the village. On the way he sees a side channel and heads for another village at the end of it.

Because Captain Carson was not committed to his goal, he went part way and then changed course. Because Captain Brown's reason to go was not strong, he gave up at the first sign of trouble.

Sometimes we do the same thing. We may set a goal to play a sport or to take a course in school. If our motives are not strong enough, we may drop out or change our mind in midstream.

If we have strong reasons for our decisions, we can do much more than we think we can. Captain Jones sailed on because people were hungry and he had food. If you have a strong reason, the storms or problems of life won't be able to stop you.

Setting goals is easy. All you have to do is make a list or even simply say, "I want to do such and such." What makes a goal easy to fulfill is a good solid motive and drive behind it. We'll discuss how to develop that drive with the help of your value system and management skills.

WE LIVE IN TIME

Before you can set goals, you need to understand the set of values you live by. People rarely fulfill goals that do not fit into their value system. For example, if it is part of your value system not to steal, you won't be very happy about a goal to rob a bank.

That sounds obvious, but many of our values are so much a part of us that we don't always realize they are there. For example, we may value time spent with a friend more than time spent with a brother or sister. Or the reverse may be true.

By understanding your values, it becomes easier to give purpose and meaning to the goals you set. Let's look at specific cases.

Time is something that must always be considered when setting goals. We live in time, and our society

---

Parents, other family members, or counselors can help you set realistic goals.

operates within time frames. Therefore time must be included within the framework of a goal.

No matter what goal you set, it will take time to fulfill it. Some goals take a short time, like losing five pounds of weight or winning a school election. Others may take a long time, such as losing 100 pounds or finishing high school.

Because time is involved, it must be considered when setting a goal. You must decide whether your goal is worth the necessary time. This is where your value system comes into play.

If you are losing five pounds so you can fit into tighter pants or impress your friends, that may or may not fit into your value system. If it is to impress people whom you don't really like but who are popular in school, you can see the conflict already. Because you don't like the people, you are not likely to try as hard to fulfill the goal.

If, however, the doctor tells you to lose 100 pounds or you will be very sick or die, you have a strong motive that fits into your value system. Most of us value life. Most of us value good health. We would want to fulfill a goal that would keep us alive and healthy.

Some people do not value life very much. They may be in deep depression or feel that they don't want to live. In that case the doctor's warning would not motivate them to diet. They would not bother spending the time they had left thinking about what they ate.

Any goal you set will take time to fulfill. Therefore, consider carefully whether the goal fits into
your value system. Next think of your purpose. Is
your goal worth spending that time on? Will you
give up time with friends or family to accomplish it?
Will it take time away from other important things?

If you wanted to be a top basketball player and set
that as your goal, it would take a lot of your time.
You would need to practice several hours a day.
That might be fine, but would doing so interfere
with other goals? What if you also wanted to graduate from high school? If the basketball practice took
time from homework, there would be a conflict of
interests. You would have to study your values and
decide which goal was more important to you.

Once the value of time is decided upon, it is easier
to set and stick to your goals.

CHAPTER

2

THE ROLE OF VALUES

Families and friends are the most important people in our lives. Since we value them, we need to consider them when setting goals. If a goal takes us away from them, we have to decide whether the goal is worth it. Perhaps your family or friends are not so important. In that case you may *want* to set goals that take you away.

For example, let's look at the goal to join the armed forces. Once you finished school you would have to leave home to serve on a military base. Some armed forces personnel serve overseas. You would have to decide which meant more to you, staying close to family and friends or going away to serve your country.

You may want to plan your goals so there is time for your friends and family.

If you were in an abusive home or your parents were alcoholics, leaving home would be a strong motive.

Some men and women, on the other hand, can't bear to move away from family and friends, and therefore change their minds about the armed forces. For example, during the war with Iraq many women who joined the armed forces after high school later found they didn't want to go to Saudi Arabia because they had babies at home. Their goal to be in the armed forces conflicted with their ideas about being mothers.

Some goals need to be thought out because they can destroy family relationships. Some goals strengthen them. One teen may decide to work at McDonald's after school in order to help with the family finances. Another teen may do so to save money to buy clothes to impress friends at school.

The teen working to help his or her family is more likely to fulfill the goal to work. That is because of the motive behind it, which involves the value placed on the family.

Sometimes teenagers have goals set for them by their families. The success in reaching these goals depends on what the teen feels is more important—family expectations or personal needs. Consider the father who wants his son to go into the family business or the teenage girl who is pressured to date a family friend. In both cases, the teenagers will follow through on these goals only if they value family approval.

If you have strong family ties or strong ties to your friends, your goals should revolve around them. It would be unwise to consider goals that would take you away from them or make them turn away from you.

For example, if your family has high ethical values and does not approve of premarital sex, your goal not to have sex before marriage will fit in with your family's values. They will support you in your goal and do everything they can to help you fulfill it.

If, on the other hand, you were more interested in pleasing your girlfriend or boyfriend and set a goal to do what he or she wanted, you could run into problems. First, the premarital sex would conflict with the values you were taught. Second, your family would be more likely to try to stop you. If you loved your family, this conflict would make it very difficult.

You can see that your relations with family and friends need to be considered before you set your goals. You need to try to set goals that won't bring you into conflict with your feelings for family and friends.

WHY WE NEED GOALS

Our culture places a high value on education. Most success in our society is measured by how much education we have. Most jobs require a high school diploma.

When setting goals, you need to know how you value education. If it is important to you, your goals must not interfere with your schooling. If education holds no special value for you, it probably will not be considered when making goals.

If a teen wants to be a star football player and sets that as his goal, he must consider his education. Most schools require a C or better average in order to play on a school team. If the person does not want to commit to doing homework or studying for tests, he should not set a goal to be a football star.

Goals that involve school are often difficult to make because it is harder to see the value. Many

Spending time on studies in school will lead to more options later in life.

courses required in school don't seem to relate to real life. Their purpose is not clear. That is why many teenagers have a hard time setting a goal to finish high school. They won't work at something they don't believe in.

One must look for and see the value of education in order to make success in school a goal. Having money is part of status in our society, but so is education. If you want to be an accepted part of middle-class or upper-class America, you must have an education.

A high-school dropout who is a drug dealer, for example, can have lots of money. He will never be accepted because he is not educated. But there are other reasons for his not being accepted. Dealing drugs does not fit into our system of values and ethics, and it tears down the community.

A high-school dropout rarely lives a "successful" life because he had not met our culture's demand for education. Of course, there are exceptions. Some teens drop out of school and then later reset their goals. They may go to night school, or get special training while they work.

Before you set goals, you need to know whether you value education and why. Then you can set goals that fit into your value system.

Every culture or society has an economic system. Our society has a high standard of living. In order to be in the middle or upper classes, you not only need an education, but also a job that is accepted as serving society's needs.

Some jobs that are highly valued do not pay high salaries. Teachers, politicians, members of the clergy are highly valued. Their jobs require a lot of education, but they are not wealthy by our standards. Some jobs, such as union labor, pay well but require no more than a high school diploma.

All jobs that are acceptable provide a service to the community. Being a waitress or maid or gas station attendant may not be high-status jobs, but they are important to the economy. We need the services. Therefore, even though the pay may not be high, the jobs are acceptable.

When you consider what goals you want to set in regard to jobs or your career, you need to think about where you want to stand in society. If you want to be upper-middle class, you need to set goals in education and career that will put you in that position.

If wealth or class mean little to you, you have more options in finding work. You should look for something you enjoy doing. Remember the need for purpose? You will never achieve a goal to move up in the world if that goal holds no value for you. There will be too many rough times and storms to weather.

To set goals regarding jobs or career, you need to look at your values of time, family, friends, school, and society. Once you have done that, you can set goals in the order you need to achieve them. With your value system supporting you, success will be more likely.

MANAGEMENT OF TIME

It is important to understand the management needed to set and fulfill goals. Values need to be considered. Family and friends influence choices. Your role in school and society must be thought out.

Once you understand what is involved in managing a goal, it will be easier for you to set the goal and fulfill it. All areas must be taken into account.

Chapter One discussed how time must be considered in setting a goal. It is especially important to consider it when you plan the management of your goal. First you need to set priorities for your time. In other words, list your goals and activities in the order of importance. When that is done, figure out how much time each goal will require.

It is important to balance time for school work with other interests and goals.

For example, if you want to quit smoking you can set a time frame within which to do it. If you smoke a pack of cigarettes a day, the first step might be to cut back to half a pack, then to a quarter pack, until finally the big day when you don't smoke even one cigarette.

Many teens and adults make the mistake of not giving themselves enough time to accomplish a goal. They decide they want something, and thinking about it makes them want it that very moment. Patience is one of the most important qualities to have when setting goals.

A person who does not set aside enough time to reach a goal soon becomes frustrated and gives up before having a chance to fulfill the goal. Remember the ship captains in the introduction? Captain Carson set out for the village. He even weathered the storm. Yet he got impatient, and instead of taking time to get to the village, he turned down a nearer channel.

If you set a goal to work at a summer job so you can buy a car in the fall, you have set up a time frame. You expect to earn money to buy the car in three months. Before you set that time frame, you need to be sure it is reasonable. Can you get a summer job? Can you find one that pays enough to cover the cost of a car? Have you considered other expenses you'll have during the summer, such as dates, clothes, entertainment, and gifts?

Perhaps you have figured in all of these factors. You have a job that will pay what you need. Your other expenses are covered. Then you are likely to achieve your goal.

It also helps to be flexible. What if an emergency comes up? Say your brother has an accident and you need to give your parents some of your pay to help with expenses. That will set your goal back. You won't have the money.

Again, priorities must be considered. Is it more important to you to help your brother or to have the car by the fall? Because you probably value your brother's well-being, you can change your time frame and buy the car in December instead. Being flexible can save you frustration and give you peace of mind.

If, however, you keep blowing your savings on parties, you've allowed too much flexibility in your time. You may never save the money for a car unless you control your actions. Consider your priorities. Ask yourself which is more important—saving to buy the car or having fun now.

GOALS AFFECT RELATIONSHIPS

Since we live with others, they must also be considered when setting goals. Most teens live with their families. Before they set a goal they need to be aware of how fulfilling that goal will affect the other members of the family.

If you set a goal to have your own bedroom by your sixteenth birthday, you have to understand how that will affect everyone. If you share a bedroom now, where will the other person go? Does your family have room in the house for you to achieve this goal?

Perhaps you know that your family's goal is to move into a bigger house by the time you are sixteen. If that is so, your goal to have your own room

Your goals may affect other members of your family. You may depend on family members to help you realize your goals.

is reasonable. If, however, your family lives in a four-bedroom house and you have six brothers and sisters, your goal may be unreasonable.

Almost any goal you set will affect those around you. If you decide to diet, other family members will have to watch what they eat in front of you. If your goal is to get better grades, your family and friends will have to allow you time to yourself so you can study. If you want to excel in a sport, your family will have to get used to your coming home late from the gym. Your friends will have to know that you can't spend time with them.

If you don't plan for the needs of family and friends when you set your goals, you can hurt your efforts. Friends who drop by when you should be studying or practicing can tempt you to go with them instead. Then you will be like Captain Carson and not achieve your goal.

It is best to include your family and friends in the planning stages of setting your goal. If you explain to them why you set the goal and how important it is to you, they will be more helpful. Let them work out schedules so they won't interfere with your time frames. Get them on your side so they can encourage you rather than hinder your progress.

Your family and friends can and should be your allies in all your ventures. Part of living and caring for others is wanting to see them succeed. Goals are hard enough to achieve on your own. With family and friends to support you, your chances of success are greater.

PLANNING GOALS AROUND SCHOOL AND WORK

Most of your teen years are spent in school. Since so much of your time revolves around school, it should be considered when planning your goals. Will your goals interfere with your school work? Will school interfere with your goals? A yes answer to either question could doom you to failure.

Many states have laws that require you to attend school until a certain age. Some states require you to have passing grades before you can get a driver's license. If you live in one of those states and your goal is to get your driver's license when you're sixteen, school is going to be a major factor.

Many schools require you to have passing grades to enter sports. If your goal is to be a tennis champ, you need to consider school.

Our culture values education. Success is largely measured by how much education you have. Most jobs require high school graduation. Therefore, it is important to set your goals around your schooling.

If you set a goal that does not give you time to study, you could have a problem. For example, say you wanted to buy a car and you got a terrific job that paid well. But what if the job required you to work long hours after school and on weekends? Or what if it were a night job? How would that affect your schoolwork?

When you start considering family, friends, and school in your planning, you can see the need for setting priorities. What is more important to you? The car? The job? Your education? Time then becomes important. Right now the car may seem most desirable. After all, it would be much more fun to cruise around town with your friends than to study. But if you consider the future you know you will need your education to become a solid citizen.

Goals that concern school must take into account the school system. If you want to study music, you need to look into what programs your school offers. If your desire is to learn drums and no one in the school can teach you drums, you will have to change your goal or find someone outside of school to teach you.

A student who wants to study cosmetology can do so in some high-school districts. Before you set

—

Many school activities provide experience for careers and goals later in life.

that goal, you would need to discover if your district offered it. If not, you might have to bring time into play and wait until you graduated from high school so you could take classes at a junior college. Or perhaps the junior college offers programs for high-school students.

When these kinds of problems arise, school counselors and teachers can be a big help. Like your family and friends, most educators are eager to help. Get them on your side and you will find it easier to manage your goals.

Your financial status is always a big factor in managing your goals. Before setting any goal, it is wise to check whether it is financially possible. You cannot set a goal to buy a car if you don't have the means to get the money for it.

Since most teens live at home, it is also a must to include your family in the discussion of finances. If you want to take those drum lessons and the school doesn't offer them, private lessons will be needed. You can tell your folks you'll pay for them out of the money you earn at your part-time job. But what if your family counts on you to help pay some of the family bills?

Before setting any goals, cost must be figured. Not only the initial cost, but the ongoing cost. You may have the money to buy a car, but can you pay for the insurance and license fees? Your parents may even buy you a car, but if they expect you to buy gas and maintain the car, can you do so?

Most things we want to do or have cost money. Material things usually involve the cost of upkeep and maintenance. These costs all must be considered or you will fail before you fulfill your goal.

Captain Brown, in our introduction, weighed the cost of losing his ship in the storm against the purpose of his goal. Since he was just sightseeing, he did not consider the goal of seeing the village worth the expense of possibly crashing on the rocks.

Captain Jones, on the other hand, felt that the lives of the villagers were more important than the possible expense. His value system told him to risk the ship to get food to the starving villagers.

When considering your goals, you need to take into account the time required to achieve them. You must consider the cost. Both of these factors must be considered in relation to your family, friends, and school. It is best to include these people in your planning to insure success.

Once you have considered all of these factors, you can be assured you have done your best to manage the fulfilling of your goals. Put them in priority and begin to take action. Having goals is the first step. Planning them is the second. Acting on them carries you through to success.

THE PROCESS OF SETTING GOALS

When you come to understand your values and have planned how you will manage your goals, it is time to actually set them. It helps to write them down on paper because doing so focuses your ideas. The written words will give power to succeed.

Making lists helps you to set your priorities. First make a list of everything you want, and then a list of everything you need. That includes what material things you need or desire and what things you need or want to do.

Needs are defined as anything you must have in order to survive. You *need* healthful food. You may *want* a chocolate sundae. You will die without healthful food. You will not die without a chocolate sundae.

Planning ahead will make your journey through life more satisfying.

Shelter is another need. You need a place that is safe and that protects you from the weather. A house is a need, but your own bedroom is a want.

The way to check between a need and a want is to decide whether you can live without it. If you can survive without it, it's a want. If not, it's a need.

After you have made the two lists, study them and put them in order of priority. Needs come first, since you must have them to survive. If you are homeless, your first goal is to find shelter, not to go to school or have a new dress.

If you have many needs, it is best to focus on those. If your needs are already met, it's time to move on to the wants. Because wants are not needed to survive, it is wise for you to consider them carefully.

The best way to plan what goals to set is to look at your values. Which wants are most important to you? Remember to consider time, family, friends, school, and finances. You may want very much to buy a car. If, however, that will take time away from school or you don't have the money for upkeep and insurance, you may have to move the desire for a car lower on your list. In that case, a part-time job might go higher on the list so you can earn the money to maintain a car.

Values are important, but so is management. Success comes when goals are well planned. You can want something with your whole heart, but if it is impossible for you to manage, it might be best to put it low on the list.

Some items that are not top priority may end up first because they are easier to manage. You may think finishing high school is the most important need. That, however, takes three to four years. Another goal, such as mountain bicycle racing, may be lower priority, but you can manage it now. In that case it can go to the top of the list as long as it does not interfere with the more important goal of finishing high school. If the bicycling begins to keep you from doing your homework, you'll have to think again about your goals and their order on your list.

The last thing to consider when setting a goal is the motive behind it. This ties in with values but goes deeper into need against want. Take the goal of owning a car; if you need the car to get to work, you will be more willing to give up things for it than if you just want it to cruise around in.

That is called *motivation.* Your motive or reason to set the goal is a very important factor in carrying it out.

Learning a second language is very hard to do. A person may want to learn Japanese, but because it is so difficult the motive must be strong. Students who take a second language in school but never plan to live in that country will have a very low success rate. They may be able to memorize words and grammar for tests, but they probably won't be able to speak the language or understand it well.

A student who is living in Japan, however, or lives with Japanese people who don't speak English, has a strong motive to learn the language. The student living in Japan especially will want to know the language to be able to talk to other people.

Many American schools have students from foreign countries. For example, in the Southwest many teens move from Mexico or other Latin American countries and speak only Spanish. Have you noticed how within a year these students can function using English? The American students, however, take Spanish in school for four years and still are not fluent.

The reason is simple and has nothing to do with how smart you are. It involves motivation. American students don't need Spanish to survive unless they live in a border town. The Spanish-speaking students *do* need to learn English to survive. The motivation is strong.

When the motive for goals is strong, success is strong. If you have no strong motive for fulfilling a goal, you can easily be sidetracked. Remember Captain Jones? His motive for getting to the village was strong. He needed to feed starving people.

Once your goals are listed in the order you can achieve them, the next thing is to write them down. You know people make lists of resolutions on New Year's Day. It is not just superstition. There is a good sound reason to write out your goals.

For some of you, making a graph or chart will be more meaningful than writing lists. Graphs can show your time frame as well as your goals. Charts can be filled in as you fulfill each step.

If you have a computer you can enter your goals
and revise them as you fulfill each step. Many soft-
ware companies sell programs that contain ways to
set goals and get them in order.

A calendar can help, especially for short-term
goals. If you mark the day you expect to complete
a goal, the daily reminder helps urge you on.

Graphing, charting, filing, computing, or writing
goals makes them clear and well understood. If you
want a car, don't just say I want a car. Put down on
paper the kind of car you want, the year, the make,
the model. Put down the price range you can afford
or want to pay. You can also list the color. When

**Taking note of your failures as well as your achievements will
help you to better reach your goals.**

you do that, you set your mind in motion to find exactly what you want. We shall discuss how that works in the next chapter.

When your list or chart is written, put it where you can see it every day. Some people use a wall calendar, others use a datebook. The constant re-minder keeps your mind programmed to do what you want to do. Be sure to share your goals with the family members or friends who may be affected by them.

Not all goals need to be shared, however. Some goals are best kept quiet so that negative attitudes won't influence you. For example, if you want to be a famous movie star or rock singer, that goal is best kept quiet until you are ready to act on it. You don't want anyone to laugh at your dreams or say you're silly to have them. If enough people said that, you might start to believe them.

When it is time to go to acting school or take guitar lessons, then you'll need to begin sharing the goal, but only with those involved. If you need your parents to help pay for acting lessons, they'll need to know why you want them. If your friends don't need to know, don't tell them unless they will be a support group for you.

There are many other helpful hints for setting goals. If you find some that work, hold onto them. Methods that fail should be tossed out. Goals can be achieved if you use common sense in setting them.

ACTING UPON
YOUR GOALS

It is one thing to set goals, but to achieve them one must act upon them. That means you must believe you are going to fulfill the goal and then do what needs to be done.

Many people set goals but fail to fulfill them because they don't act upon them. It takes a strong will to fulfill a goal. Captain Jones faced danger yet sailed on in spite of the rocks in the channel and the raging storm. He set aside his fears and willed his crew to push onward.

When you start off toward your goals, many things will come up that get in the way. It takes a strong will to overcome those setbacks and move on toward the goal.

Graduating from high school will be a goal full of obstacles. You might get a tough math class in which you need to study extra hours. You might miss most of a semester because of illness. If your will to get the diploma is strong enough you can overcome such problems and graduate.

Temptation is another obstacle that teens must deal with. The present desire may outweigh the long-term wish to fulfill your goal. If a girl vows not to have sexual intercourse until she marries, her goal will be put to the test many times. Dates with handsome young men, peer pressure, and her own body's desires will make it seem more desirable to have sex now.

Because of setbacks and obstacles you need to develop a strong will. You also need to have faith that your goals can be fulfilled. The girl who wants to be a famous movie star will never be one unless she believes deep in her heart that she can. The girl who wants to remain a virgin until marriage never will unless she honestly believes she can.

Faith in yourself and your beliefs is one of the strongest tools you have for success. Movies and news reports daily tell of people overcoming great odds to fulfill a dream or a goal that seemed impossible. The impossible is possible if you believe hard enough.

What often happens is that when you've set your goal your mind kicks into action for you. One of the things it does is to check for information you need. There is so much in the world for you to respond to that your mind filters out much information and lets in only what you need.

Overcoming obstacles is always a part of achieving success.

To understand that, try sitting in a park with some friends. While you are talking, try to notice everything around you: the kids playing, the cars passing, an airplane overhead, birds singing, a ball flying through the air, and your friends' voices. Your brain, unless you tell it otherwise, will block out everything except your friends because they are the ones you want to hear.

If you program your brain to pick up something else, it will. Say, for example, you hope your boyfriend will cruise by in his red car. Your mind will watch for a red car and interrupt your conversation if it sees one.

Have you ever noticed what happens when you decide to buy something, say a new bicycle? For weeks you haven't noticed that much about bicycles. But as soon as you set a goal to purchase one, your mind clicks into action.

Your mind starts sifting through information and tuning in to everything about bicycles. Your interest level builds up, and suddenly you notice every ad on TV and in the paper. You start reading bicycle magazines. Most of your conversation with friends is about bicycles.

As soon as you buy the bicycle, however, your interest drops off. You stop noticing ads. Your full attention is turned to the next goal.

Your mind helps guide you toward your goal. If you have decided to lose 20 pounds, your mind warns you when you reach for a candy bar. It helps you put your actions into gear for your goal.

This wonderful help that your mind gives you is the main reason for writing out your goals. That way your mind can be more helpful because the directions are clear. The girl in the park who is looking for her boyfriend knows that his car is red. Her mind will pick out only red cars. If she didn't know the car was red, her mind would be searching all cars and thus not be able to pay attention to her friends' conversation.

Your body, your mind, and your spirit need to work together to fulfill a goal. Your body has to be able to do it physically. If you want to be a swimming champ, you have to have a body that can swim. Your mind has to be willing to make you swim every day for practice. You won't become a champ if your will is not set.

Your spirit gives you the fire and belief that you can do it. If you feel a burning desire to be a champ, and know deep inside that you can do it, you will.

Setting and fulfilling a goal is like those ships sailing through dangerous waters. First you need to know where you are going, what the actual goal is. Next you need to have the time and means to reach it. When all the conditions are met, you can begin to take action.

You will know it is the right goal at the right time and that your plans are right if you feel at peace. If there is confusion or doubt, your goals have little chance of success. When there is strong faith and belief in yourself, your values, and your purpose, you will feel the strength of peace and will more than likely succeed.

Fulfilling goals is the means we humans use to measure our worth and success. If you want to feel positive about yourself, set reasonable goals that you can fulfill and then go for them. If you want to feel like a worthwhile citizen of your culture and community, set goals based on the values of your culture and you will be counted as successful.

The most important thing to remember when setting a goal is to set it, believe in it, and act upon it. Every person can fulfill goals that are made from the heart.

GLOSSARY
EXPLAINING NEW WORDS

cosmetology Business of beauty treatment of the skin, hair, and nails.

culture The beliefs, values, and ways of living of a particular group, such as Americans.

economics Science relating to material needs, goods and services.

ethics Matters of good and evil; moral duty.

flexible Capable of being changed.

frustrate To block something one is trying to do.

goal Something to achieve; the aim or end result toward which to work.

management The act of handling matters to achieve an end.

motive Something that causes a person to act.

obstacle Something that stands in the way of action.

options Choices one can make about courses of action, such as a career.

priority Order of importance.

temptation The act of enticing to do wrong.

values Principles or ideals that are desired.

FOR FURTHER READING

Fiction

Crutchen, Chris. *Running Loose*. New York: Greenwillow Books, 1983.

Dygrad, Thomas J. *Soccer Duel*. New York: William Morrow & Co., 1981.

Greene, Constance. *Alexandra the Great*. New York: Viking Press, 1982.

Head, Ann. *Mr. and Mrs. Bo Jo Jones*. New York: Putnam, 1967.

Love, Sandra. *Crossing Over*. New York: Lathrop, Lee & Shephard Books, 1981.

Lypsyte, Robert. *One Fat Summer*. New York: Harper & Row, 1977.

McCaffrey, Anne. *Dragon Song*. New York: Atheneum, 1976.

Mendonca, Susan. *Tough Choices*. New York: Dial Press, 1980.

Pfeffer, Susan Beth. *Starring Peter and Leigh*. New York: Delacorte Press, 1979.

Pfeffer, Susan Beth. *What Do You Do When Your Mouth Won't Open?* New York: Delacorte Press, 1981.

Sweeney, Joyce. *Dream Collector*. New York: Delacorte Press, 1989.

Sweeney, Joyce. *Right Behind the Rain*. New York: Delacorte Press, 1987.

Voight, Cynthia. *The Runner*. New York: Atheneum, 1985.

Nonfiction

Arnold, John D. *Make Up Your Mind*. New York: Amacon, 1978.

Ayer, Eleanor. *Determination*. New York: Rosen Publishing Group, 1991.

Cohen, Susan and Daniel. *Teenage Stress*. New York: M. Evans & Co., Inc., 1984.

Goldberg, Lazer. *Learning to Choose*. New York: Charles Scribner & Sons, 1976.

Hartley, Fred. *Dare to Be Different*. Old Tappen, NJ: Fleming H. Revell Co., 1980.

Johnson, Linda Carlson. *Responsibility*. New York: Rosen Publishing Group, 1991.

Klein, David and Mary Mae. *Yourself Ten Years From Now*. New York: Harcourt Brace Jovanovich, Inc., 1977.

London, Kathleen. *Who Am I? Who Are You?* Menlo Park, CA: Addison-Wesley, 1983.

McFarland, Rhoda. *Coping Through Assertiveness*. New York: Rosen Publishing Group, 1986.

McGuire, Paula. *Putting it Together*. New York: Delacorte Press, 1987.

Milhaly, Mary E. *Getting Your Own Way*. New York: M. Evans & Co., Inc., 1979.

Smith, Sandra Lee. *Value of Self-Control*. New York: Rosen Publishing Group, 1991.

Sullivan, Mary Beth, Alan J. Brightman, Joseph Blatt. *Feeling Free*. Menlo Park, CA: Addison-Wesley, 1979.

Thomas, Alicia. *Self-Esteem*. New York: Rosen Publishing Group, 1991.

INDEX

About the Author

For twenty-one years, Sandra Lee Smith has taught grades from kindergarten through college level in California and Arizona.

Active on legislative committees and in community projects, she has helped design programs to involve parents in the education process.

In response to the President's Report, *A Nation at Risk*, Ms. Smith participated in a project involving Arizona State University, Phoenix Elementary School District, and an inner-city community in Phoenix. Participants in the project developed a holistic approach to education.

Photo Credits

Page 4: AP/Wide World Photos; All other photos on cover and in book by Mary Lauzon.

Design & Production: Blackbirch Graphics, Inc.